ON BREAD & POETRY

ON BREAD & POETRY

A Panel Discussion With Gary Snyder, Lew Welch & Philip Whalen

Edited by Donald Allen

Grey Fox Press
Bolinas · California

Library of Congress Cataloguing in Publication Data

Snyder, Gary
    On bread & poetry.

    1. Poets, American—20th century—Interviews.
I. Welch, Lew, joint author. II. Whalen, Philip, joint author.
III. Title.
PS129.S6   1977   811'.5'409   77-1266
ISBN 0-912516-27-5 pbk.

Grey Fox Press books are distributed by Book People, 2940 Seventh
Street, Berkeley, California 94710.

CONTENTS

Editor's Note   vii

Lew Welch: Manifesto: Bread vs. Mozart's Watch   x

Three Broadsides

    Gary Snyder: Nanao Knows   xiii
    Lew Welch: Step Out Onto the Planet   xiv
    Philip Whalen: Three Mornings   xv

On Bread & Poetry   1

Gary SNYDER
Lew WELCH
Philip WHALEN

in 'FREEWAY'

a reading of new poems

Friday, June 12; 8:30 pm $1.00 admission

PLMA Hall, 150 Golden Gate

SAN FRANCISCO

In the winter of 1964 Henry Rago accepted four of Lew Welch's *Hermit Poems* for publication in *Poetry* (Chicago), and on May 31st Welch wrote to give him his new Mill Valley address and recent news of the Bay Area:

Dear Mr. Rago,   Gary Snyder is back from Japan for a while & we have organized a giant reading as per the attached [handbill]. The hall is the funky old place where Harry Bridges won the coast & has a monstrous mural (very well done) showing policemen beating women and children to death—the fuzz mounted on horses with hooves like Percherons, which hooves are crushing the heads of brave men etc. Nobody knows who painted it. When we asked: "Nobody knows. Except it was some Wobbly Lady from Seattle."

San Francisco and the Bay Area grow more responsive to poetry every day. Gary, Phil Whalen and I have been on the radio (FM), the *Chronicle* loves us (maybe a whole column by Ralph Gleason, local jazz column writer & very good man), everyone very excited. I predict 1,000 souls.

"You guys come on like scholars. No shit, for a long time I thought you were putting us on, like maybe you were a road cast from *Evergreen Review* or something, the real Lew Welch in the woods, Snyder still in Japan, Whalen safe and hiding."

This from [Jack Nessel] the man at KPFA (FM) after our interview & indicative of the general problem & cause for real hope.

General Problem: big fear/hate thing called war between hip & square. Poet seen as frightening hippydip. Incommunicable (poets!) folks who mumble, snarl, etc. etc.

Cause for Real Hope: All folks delighted by actual article. Express huge need for Poetry. Prove this by quick pickup of the poems (in this town you can hardly get a 50 line structure out, out loud, for interference of shrieks of laughter, cheers, etc.).

For all the reasons we all know (and which, I say, we must forget—no blame, as *I Ching* says) the whole thing got hopelessly fucked up. Ginsberg in NY beautifully correcting things. We 3 (and dozens of others) here in SF also putting it right. Or trying to.

And, weirdly, all this is happening without any real change in approach. The poems are actually tougher. I wear long hair and black boots. Why not? I'm handsome and vain. Snyder has a beard, patched jeans, a wild little over-the-shoulder black Jap bag thing. Of course! Poets have to carry books, mss, all manner of clumsy articles. Whalen wears funky old over-all-type jeans, immaculately clean, simply because he's portly & can't make it in Levi's & he's poor, terribly poor . . . . . .

How to say anything without causing a new confusion. That's what actually went wrong. One answer. Write more. Write more accurately. Write tough.

Every time we cheat, even unknowingly, thousands "die of our cowardice."

How great to have our job at a time like this—Eh Henry?

Lew Welch

[PS] Can't you figure a way to make this reading? Worth it. Also, June in SF unbelievable. Try. LW

Jack Nessel was the moderator of the panel discussion "On Bread & Poetry" for KPFA (FM); it was broadcast shortly before the "Freeway" reading at the Old Longshoremen's Hall in San Francisco. Don Carpenter arranged for most of the publicity, hired the hall, and had the handbill printed. The poets made huge posters which they put up about the city. Jim Hatch took the publicity photographs; we use one as the frontispiece. Four Seasons Foundation printed three poem broadsides, each in the poet's calligraphy, and sold them at the door to raise additional funds. On the night, an enthusiastic crowd of more than 800 welcomed their poets home.

We are grateful to Eric Bauersfeld of KPFA for permission to publish *On Bread & Poetry*; to Saundra Taylor, Curator of Manuscripts, The Lilly Library, Indiana University, for permission to quote at length from Lew Welch's May 31, 1964 letter to Henry Rago; and to Aram Saroyan for his careful transcription of the tape.

Donald Allen

ix

Lew Welch: Manifesto: Bread vs. Mozart's Watch

I don't think there ever really was a war between the Hip and the Square, and if there is, I won't fight in it. I am a poet. My job is writing poems, reading them out loud, getting them printed, studying, learning how to become the kind of man who has something of worth to say. It's a great job.

Naturally I'm starving to death. Naturally? No, man, it just does not make sense.

('Look, baby, you want to pay your bills, go out and get a job.')

I've got a job. I'm a Poet. Why should I do somebody else's job, too? You want me to be a carpenter? I'm a lousy carpenter. Does anybody ask a carpenter to write my poems?

But there I am, working 20 hours a day in a salmon and crab boat (a beautiful job in its own right, but another story, just as why I didn't make it that way either, is another story). And suddenly I realize I haven't made a poem in eight months. Too tired. And I still couldn't pay my bills, $125 a month in 1962 San Francisco, frugality being one of the tricks of the Poet Trade.

Meanwhile publishers ('Sorry, there's no money for the Poets') were printing my poems—big Readings got read (all Benefits, no bread) etc., etc., etc.

So I cracked up. My brain, literally, snapped under the weirdness of being a Poet, a successful one and being BECAUSE OF MY JOB (which all agree is noble and good and all that) an outcast.

PLEASE NOTE: None of this has anything to do with the Beat Generation, America, Hipness and Squareness—it's as old as Mozart. I see the basic con as: Bread vs. Mozart's Watch (don't pay the guy, that would be too vulgar a return for work so priceless. Give him a watch. Make sure the watch is engraved with a message that prevents him from pawning it.)

So as I say, I cracked up. I took myself to the woods for almost two years. I sat in a CCC shack 400 miles north of here, and did my homework. Spring water. Big beautiful Salmon River. No bills. Help from Home.

Last November I returned to this city, mostly healed. Many poems. Some new answers.

I learned a great many things up there but one of the strangest is: the plight of the Poet (in fact, the whole Mozart/Watch con) is partly our fault. THOUSANDS OF PEOPLE REALLY DO DIG OUR WORTH AND OUR WORK. THEY REALLY WANT TO HELP—AND THEY DON'T KNOW HOW!

If we're so damned Creative, we ought to be able to solve this problem for our people. And it isn't just a problem for Poets. It even gets to Ferry Boats. I refuse to believe a region this rich cannot afford Ferry Boats!

I stand for Beauty and Delight and Love and Truth in every form. I am a poet. I see, finally, that part of my job is to show how we CAN afford Poetry and Ferry Boats and good Live Jazz and Dancers and Girls in Fishbowls*—how, in fact, we can't begin to live without them. Without them the City is only a hideous and dangerous tough Big Market —of no interest and no delight and no point to anyone.

First I have to solve my problem. Without in any way causing a strain on my community, without begging or conning anyone in any way, I will pay my bills entirely by doing my real job, which is Poet.

Then I can give attention to solving more general problems—again, without strain, without begging or conning.

Charity-Crusade shots are out, for example.

On Friday, June 12th, at 8:30 at the Old Longshore-men's Hall, 150 Golden Gate Avenue, you can hear some of these discussed in my Poetry—Gary Snyder, Philip Whalen and I will read from our new work at that time.

See Utopian Visions built before your very eyes! Poems! Delights! As George Herms, local poet/sculptor said: "God says we can, Louise!"

Cheap. $1.

*The "Girl in the Fishbowl" was an attraction/illusion at Bimbo's 365 Club in San Francisco during the 1960s. Ed.

NANAO KNOWS

Mountains, cities, all so
        light, so loose. blankets
Buckets — throw away —
Work left to do.
        it doesn't last.

Each girl is real
        her nipples harden, each
                        has damp
        her smell — her hair —
— What am I to be saying.
There they all go
Over the edge, dissolving.

Rivetters bind up
Steel rod bundles
For wet concrete.
In and out of forests,
                cities, families
        like a fish.

                        25. III. 64
                        Gary Snyder

step out onto the Planet.
Draw a circle 100 feet round.

Inside the circle are 300 things
    nobody understands and,
    maybe, nobody's ever seen.

How many can you find?

Lew Welch
6/12/64

THREE MORNINGS

1.

Fog dark early morning I wait here
Half awake, shall I go back to bed
Somebody next door whistles the ST. ANTHONY CHORALE
I think of Brahms, a breakfast of hot chocolate whipcream
sweet bright pastry
bits of sugar-blossom in his beard

2.

I wait for breakfast to drop from the sky
foghorns,   clusters of churchbells
pale sun butter
traffic airplane marmalade
salt & pepper avacado branch squeak on window
I drink last night's cold tea.

3.

Clear bluey-yellow sky—a morning here.—
grey cloudbank with lights of Oakland underneath—
Baywater blacky blue   b o a t l i g h t s
ROBIN: clink clink clink clank clink
(6 ADHYOYA, BRIHADARANYAKA UPANISHAD.)

8:V:63 — 15:VII:63
Philip Whalen
San Francisco

Philip Whalen

XV

ON BREAD & POETRY

GARY SNYDER: I'm Gary Snyder. I was born in San Francisco, raised up from the age of two or so in Washington state near Seattle, in the country; went to school in Seattle, in Portland, graduated from Reed College in Portland; did a year—half a year—of linguistic study at Indiana University; then came back out to San Francisco, spent my time going to school at the University of California in the winters studying Chinese and Japanese, and spent my summers working for the Forest Service or the Park Service up in the mountains. In 1956 I went to Japan, and since that time I've lived most of the time in Japan.

LEW WELCH: I'm Lew Welch. I was born in Phoenix, Arizona, and my family sort of moved up the [California] coast, never staying anywhere longer than about two years, three years. I ended up in high school in Palo Alto, and then was in the Air Force during the war—World War II, that is—and went to Reed College, and graduated from Reed in 1950, and then made the mistake of going to the University of Chicago. All I really wanted to do was—I'd never been out of the West and I wanted to see what New York and Chicago and New Orleans looked like, for some reason. It took me eight and a half years to get back. Got hung up in Chicago where I worked for a while in the advertising world and cracked up, and then came back here. I'd say I've thought of myself as a poet since I was about twenty years old. I'm now thirty-seven. But I think I've only really admitted it to myself the last five to seven years; that is, actually, that's what I've been—it only is a poet since then. The last two years I left the San Francisco area and lived in a CCC shack up in the Marble Mountain-Trinity Alps area near Yreka. Stayed there nearly two years and I've just been back in town since December.

PHILIP WHALEN: My name is Phil Whalen and I was born in Portland and raised in The Dalles. It's about ninety miles east of Portland on the Columbia River. I moved back there when I was about seventeen-eighteen years old, back to Portland, was drafted into the army in forty-three, and got out in forty-six. I was in the old Army Air Corps as a radio operator mechanic and an instructor. After the war, I came to Reed College and graduated in fifty-one, and since then I've lived mostly in and around San Francisco, some of the time in L.A., and worked for the Forest Service, and oh, for almost two years, I worked up here in Strawberry Canyon washing laboratory glassware in the Poultry Husbandry Department of the University. And since then I've been sort of drifting, scuffling, and writing lots more poems. The first book that I got out was called *Like I Say*; it was published in 1960. And another book came out the same year called *Memoirs of an Inter-Glacial Age*. One was published in New York and one in San Francisco. And so since fifty-nine I've lived here in San Francisco fairly steadily, scuffling, and writing.

MODERATOR: You're all more or less identified in the popular imagination as members of the San Francisco Renaissance, as it was called back in the early fifties when *Howl* came out and Ginsberg named his fellows "angel-headed hipsters." Do you conceive of the poet as necessarily an outlaw in society? How do you see your role?

GARY SNYDER: I don't see my role as being any outlaw in society, but I rather look at the society and see what we have—modern Western civilization and the way that it's spreading around the world—as being an aberrant thing, an outlaw of its own sort on the planet. And so I feel more that I am trying to play a middle way—sane kind of role, holding to some balance and some measure, against what seem to me to be extreme and aberrant tendencies in the society.

I'm willing to make a living as a poet in the society, and it's up to the society whether I'm an outsider or not an outsider, that isn't my concern—I just have my work to do. Now if I can't make it as a poet and I can't live off poetry, that's all right too, I'll get by somehow. Either way.

MODERATOR: *Can* you make it as a poet? How do all of you earn your livings? How do you get bread?

WELCH: Well, I get mine in any kind of left-handed job that's left over, that nobody seems to want, and cab-driving. I've gone salmon fishing, worked in the Post Office— usually the rush times like Christmas, and so on. I won't do that any more because the FBI wants you to tell people every place you've lived and worked since you were sixteen, and I think that's ridiculous. It's none of their business. And I've moved around so much I couldn't do it anyway; on my conscience, I couldn't answer those questions—I think a lot of people are that way. And I resent being asked that. And then, after I got to be thirty-five I ran into that silly notion that's around that I was too old to do anything unless I was already doing it, and so it's becoming harder and harder for me to find work in this country that makes money.

Of course, my real work, my writing, doesn't in any way—well, I've published probably eighteen or twenty major works, and one book, and in several anthologies, and I have made less than four hundred dollars, total, off the writing itself. Possibly a hundred and fifty altogether out of readings, maybe eleven readings. You usually end up with a twenty dollar bill. And recently I got so tired of all this that that's the main reason I went up to live in the woods where things are cheap. I had a rent-free place, no utilities bill, free spring water, and I sat down and thought and thought about this problem, not only from the standpoint of my life, but the lives of my friends who want to make it as a poet, or dancer, or musician—it doesn't really matter what they are, they aren't getting paid. For example, the girl in the fishbowl, at Bimbo's, in San Francisco is one of the most beautiful things about the city, and she gets *fifteen dollars a night*. Now the bartender, who is just a bartender, gets about twenty-two-fifty—I don't think that's fair.

SNYDER: It takes more skill for him to do what he's doing. [Laughter.]

WELCH: Well, possibly, but she's more important to our community, I'm quite sure.

SNYDER: Listen, Lew, do you think you have any occupational skills now that you could live off of?

WELCH: Well, that was a mistake I made early in my life—if I had it to do over again, I'd make very sure I had some skills such as the printing trade, or some such trade . . .

SNYDER: Some kind of trade, you mean . . .

WELCH: Some kind of trade where by this time I would have a technical proficiency in something. Well, while I was growing up my job always seemed to me to be to get myself into the kind of person that would have something interesting and accurate to say about things. And in order to develop into that kind of person, I always found it exciting and interesting to change jobs a lot, to do a lot of different kinds of things, and I always like working with my hands—just labor jobs. I *preferred* them to these high pressure, often very trivial and frustrating office type jobs; and bureaucracies always have horrified me, I just *can't* get involved with that kind of nonsense.

MODERATOR: If you were to work in a trade, you'd probably be subject to regular hours, and how would you react to that?

WELCH: Well, that's the trouble there too. It takes me, really—well, it's like Gertrude Stein said, she said you may only write a half an hour a day but you spend all day getting ready for that half hour. And I find when I have a full-time, five, six-day-a-week job, eight hours a day, I, in a very short time, am getting no writing done at all. A period of two or three months is enough to just shut it off entirely.

MODERATOR: Phil Whalen—you've published widely, and you've worked around—how long on the average does it take you to write something that you're fully satisfied with, and how much do you generally get paid when it's finally published?

WHALEN: Oh, sometimes a completely satisfactory poem can be done in about two minutes, and then other times it takes three-four years to get the thing completely there and it just takes a while to arrive. And then often I am asked to contribute—I usually contribute to whatever magazine asks me, and usually they don't pay. The most I think that I've got for any [laughs] single piece of writing is some place around, oh, thirty-forty dollars, something like that. But, as far as working goes, I don't mind doing a part-time job ordinarily. Well, like when I was working here in Berkeley that glass job was a part-time deal. It was very good because it was four hours a day and the rest of the time I had off—I could sleep, and walk around, and read, and it was fine. Right now I'm sort of getting by on my pretty face [laughs] more than anything else, and it's a great burden on my nerves, but the thing that's important to me is that I have a great deal to write right now, and I'm writing it down, and it's very expensive, and what not, and it's too bad.

MODERATOR: When you work is there a separation of what you're doing for a living and your writing that bugs you?

WHALEN: No, no . . .

MODERATOR: Is anybody bugged by that?

WHALEN: Not any more, not since—oh, goodness, not since I was a boy and had jobs. Before I was in the Army, I was an office boy or something like that where it was a steady eight-hour-a-day job in a deal that I didn't like and I didn't have sense enough to stop [laughs]. Or being in the Army itself was a big drag, having to do a whole lot of crummy things, take a lot of bad orders. But that was a definite split that I had a hard time sewing up but I've gradually, I think, fixed it up so that there isn't any split anymore between what I think and what I'm doing and what I want, and so forth. It's all evening out, slowly. But then, I'm also nearly forty-one years old—it's taken a long time to do.

SNYDER: Yeah . . . Well, ever since I realized that you don't have to write like an Oxford don to be poet . . .

MODERATOR: Yeah? . . . [laughing]

SNYDER: . . . I've had no problem at all. Whatever work I've done, whatever job I've had, has fed right into my poetry, and it's all in there.

MODERATOR: You've traveled all through Japan. How do you support yourself when you're traveling?

SNYDER: Well, I haven't traveled in Japan, I've lived in one place in Japan, actually; and over there I supported myself initially by doing some paid research and translation work, and then later I got into the English conversation teaching business for companies. The rapidly expanding economy of Japan demands that they have a lot of interaction and trade contact with European countries and America. The English language is the medium for this, and the Japanese people have had a hard time picking up on spoken English, so that English teachers are very much in demand right now, and it's a very good gig—they pay well, and the hours are not long.

WHALEN: That's a more interesting split, talk about language, than that between working and living. One thing we've all been hung up on—anybody who lives in this country, who writes, has been hung up on—is the split between writing English, as Gary was saying a minute ago, as an Oxford don, and writing as an American, writing in the way that we speak, writing the language that is live, that is actually spoken. And that creates considerable mental tension that makes it hard for us to write, but which settles itself out slowly.

MODERATOR: Is there an academic style that you're resisting?

SNYDER: There's an academic style and an academic language, which is literary, poetic, and so forth, and it doesn't come from the way anybody around here speaks, and it doesn't have much to do with the way anybody is living.

To take older, and well-beaten examples—John Crowe Ransom, Allen Tate, the Cornbelt Metaphysicals, as Rexroth would say. But there's plenty of younger ones, in the universities, although now the thing that is developing, curiously enough, is a kind of academicized William Carlos Williams thing, that they're picking up on finally.

MODERATOR: This is becoming institutionalized in the academies?

SNYDER: Yeah, that's becoming institutionalized too. Anyway, what we call British English is—it's not exactly British English, but what literary writing is, is closer to British English, and very few people yet have really gotten into writing American American.

WHALEN: Yeah, the *New Yorker*, I suppose, is the thing that's sitting there trying to be American British English, and peddles that weekly from their little hole there in New York.

WELCH: And, you see, in our work, not just the three of us but there is a wonderfully large group of serious American poets now who are writing like we talk. And it's nice how many people are delighted. They say, "Well, gee, that sounds just like the way you *talk*."

WHALEN: Other people say, "It isn't a poem at all!"

WELCH: And other people say: "It can't be a poem—that just sounds like talk." This is what makes it exciting now from the standpoint of a literary movement and everything. It's a very exciting time to be an artist when a thing is coming to be. I mean we still don't know what all this stuff is going to look like because we haven't written it all yet.

SNYDER: Well, I find it very exciting to have some poems, a few poems which I can show to academic types, or say, artistic and literary types around San Francisco, and they will say, "Yes, that's a poem." And I can also read it or show it to a logger or a seaman, and he will say, "That's great. Yeah, I like that."

WELCH: Yes, that's one of my standards, too.

WHALEN: And that's something that all of us have been able to do, incidentally. I mean a lot of friends of mine have come around and said, "I showed something of yours to this bum," and so on, and the bum flipped. And it's great.

WELCH: The cab drivers like my cab poems. They said, "Yeah, that's just the way it is. By gosh, you write like that, hunh? That's good."

MODERATOR: Who are you writing for?

WHALEN: For you! [Laughs] That's who. Or for whoever will stop and look for a minute.

WELCH: Whoever's interested. To whom it may concern, you might say.

WHALEN: Whoever will bother to read it, or listen, that's

all. It's not an audience, but *persons*, like that fellow over there with the beard in the control room, or whoever's running up and down Shattuck Avenue right now.

WELCH: Or your landlady. I mean I use poetry all the time I find, not only my own but the old poets and some of my contemporaries, to say something *well* that comes up in conversation. And I say, "Well, as Yeats said, in la la la la," and so on, and I think that's the only validity poetry . . . I mean if it's really a part of your life, it greatly enriches your life. It's a nice thing to have around as part of your life. It's not, in other words, a stuffy, academic thing that you can learn *about* in a university, and then do all alone in your room, or some weird thing like some perversion. It's alive speech.

SNYDER: Well, this is the exciting thing about readings, of course, and that was one of the things that really turned us on about 1956 when we started reading poetry aloud around San Francisco, was that it reminded everybody that the excitement of poetry is a communal, social, human thing, and that poems aren't meant to be read in the quiet of your little room all by yourself with a dictionary at hand, but are something to be excitedly enjoyed in a group, and be turned on by.

WELCH: Right. To be *sung*, in a word. It can be a very nice part of life—it's like music, and dance, and everything.

SNYDER: Poetry has a very ancient ritual, magical, social function that goes back fifty thousand years.

WELCH: Sure. You would advise the Prince and do all sorts of things with it.

WHALEN: Sure. But I do think that there is a personal use also. I mean if you're feeling sad and crummy and *are* alone in your room and aren't doing anything and you pick up like a—a real good book like that Elizabethan anthology of Norman Ault, you read through some of the poems in it and you get a *lift*, you get—it's a *cure*, a turn-on. You have a line in one of your poems yourself, Gary, about, "high on poetry" . . .

WELCH: And mountains.

WHALEN: And mountains.

WELCH: Yeah. A hiking poem. Yeah. Well, you know, I was very moved, very touched when this nation was grieving the loss of President Kennedy, and the television and radio people realized how really crummy and vulgar those ads sound, and so stopped all that advertising for a minute, and tried to express this grief. One of the things that naturally came to mind is well, we ought to have some poetry, and the great actors of the United States just came on and read their favorite poems. There'd be *hours* of real poetry suddenly on *television*. And everyone seemed to appreciate that and so—now there's a real example of it, really: it was *used* by this community, the whole United States here, at a moment of great grief, in this case. Well, it can also be used in moments of elation, and other ways, and I think more and more Americans are becoming aware of this art as something that's—*enjoyable*, you know, not some distant, difficult thing.

SNYDER: Well, poetry is for the emotions too.

WELCH: Sure it is.

SNYDER: And whenever people can break through the—whatever it is that's caked-up and crusted on them so that they don't see, when they start to *feel*, poetry comes.

WELCH: That's right.

SNYDER: They read it or they hear it or they sing it.

WELCH: Or if their mind gets all cranked up on a bad problem—you can look to the wise old men, look to the old poets: what did they have to say about this?

MODERATOR: At the time when President Kennedy was assassinated there was a tendency to turn to Whitman on much of the television and radio memorials . . .

WELCH: Yes.

MODERATOR: Do you think that there could have been other choices that would have been just as apt to express the feelings?

SNYDER: Oh, he's the best, though.

WHALEN: Certainly, certainly, there are plenty of Greek poets that were great . . .

WELCH: Yes.

WHALEN: . . . which would have been even more apt, considering.

SNYDER: Yeah, but Whitman is the *American* poet.

MODERATOR: How about more contemporary poets?

SNYDER: The thing they did probably was hang up on "When lilacs last in the dooryard bloom'd, . . ."

WELCH: That's right . . . stuff like that.

SNYDER: . . . over and over again.

WHALEN: But it's very funny—all of us got letters about four or five months after the assassination . . .

WELCH: Yeah.

WHALEN: . . . from some bright young people in New York who had a publishing business and who said, "Have you written anything about the assassination, or about the life and times of JFK, and if so, would you please send it to us, and do you know anybody else who has, or might have, and so on, cause we want to make an anthology of writings about all this."

MODERATOR: Did this strike you as cheap?

WHALEN: And I wrote back and said, "No, I'm sorry, it hadn't occurred to me, I wasn't very interested in the man, I'm sorry he is dead, but . . ."

WELCH: Yeah, it didn't strike one as cheap, but I had no

poem on the subject, although I was very—you know, very upset by that, it affected me personally in a way that was quite surprising. I didn't realize I was so fond of the man. But I don't know whether it makes—I wasn't trying to make the point that the very best poetry ended up any-where, or anything. It just was nice to see people like Frederic March and everything allowed to read the poems that he'd liked all his life, you know. It became—well, like you started out with the question: "Do you feel like an outlaw?" I feel like an *outcast*, often. Not so much any-more. Possibly I'm getting more mature about it, but I do think that part of it is—America is changing. It really used to be just about worth your *life*—to say you were a *poet*, in a tough bar, say. You certainly—it's the fastest way not to get employed, to tell the personnel director, "Well, I'm a poet," and so on. Now, I've been doing it lately. I do it all the time—to my landladies over the phone if I'm trying to get a new apartment, or to people that I'm trying to get a job from, and I find their response is—oh, more than half the time it's very warm: "Oh really? Are you a poet? Oh, my goodness, what kinda poems do you write?" Blah, blah, blah, you know.

MODERATOR: Generally speaking, how do you all relate to the bulk of the people that you pass on the street, and that you talk to, who don't dress like you, who probably don't think like you, and who probably don't know very much about what you're interested in, what you're doing, and, uh, about poetry?

SNYDER: Well, in the first place, I don't think they dress so different from me. And I don't think so different from them. [Laughter.]

WELCH: No, I don't think of it as any hip-square division anymore. I really used to, and I think it was a great error . . .

WHALEN: Yeah.

WELCH: . . . on my part. I think it was not only inaccurate, but it was immoral. I mean if you start thinking of we-*them*, naturally you cause all kinds of hostilities to rise. Well, I—you know, I *like* people, I'm a very gregarious person. And it doesn't seem to—as I look over my friends, it doesn't seem to have much to do with how they dress, or what kind of a job they have. I mean some of my best friends are *ad men*, really.

MODERATOR: How did you relate to Mailer's essay, *The White Negro*? How do you view this attitude?

WELCH: Oh, I thought he had a good idea there, and kinda got it awful New York-complicated . . .

WHALEN: But anyway, as far as society and roles and what not, I really take now a very fancy view of myself. I think of myself as a poet like Homer was a poet, or like Ben Jonson was . . .

WELCH: Yes, and I do too.

WHALEN: . . . or like John Crowe Ransom or somebody, I mean that's my business; or my shape or manifestation in

this world is that. And I don't think we need any apology
or that it's a great mystery—well, it is a slight mystery
but . . .

WELCH: Yeah.

WHALEN: . . . but it's a mystery like a carpenter, in the
medieval sense . . .

SNYDER: Yeah.

WELCH: Exactly, exactly.

WHALEN: The carpenter had a mystery. He had a thing
that he could *do*—and he could do it well, and he was him-
self doing that thing. Well, I'm me doing that . . .

WELCH: Right.

WHALEN: . . . like the carpenter does, or like the doctor,
or like the engineer, or whatever.

SNYDER: I think that all of us probably would agree on
this—that we are not concerned or hung up with any hos-
tility as such, toward any particular people . . .

WHALEN: No.

WELCH: No.

SNYDER: . . . or towards society, or toward anything in
general in that way. That really isn't a worthwhile concern.

WELCH: I do have a great concern though of—a real
despair and sadness when I see so many Americans living

so *badly*.

SNYDER: But that's—that's a different thing from hating cops, you see . . .

WELCH: It certainly is an *entirely* different thing. And that got badly confused sometime around fifty-eight or nine—there was just too much of this—of a *senseless* hostility going back and forth, coming from both sides, about *nothing*.

MODERATOR: Do you find that the bulk of your poems are what might be called protest poems?

WELCH: No, not at all, not at all.

MODERATOR: Anybody?

WHALEN: No, I think of myself as a lyric poet . . .

WELCH: I do too.

WHALEN: . . . like I say, like Callimachus or something, for God's sake. It's very simple.

SNYDER: Anything that speaks truth is a protest if what's going on around it is not true.

WELCH: Exactly. Yes.

SNYDER: That's all.

WELCH: And it just isn't, it just isn't necessary . . .

SNYDER: And so in one sense maybe everything we write is protest . . .

WELCH: Sure.

SNYDER: . . . but that's not the point in writing it. What we're trying to do is stick to what seems right.

WELCH: Right. And I often find myself saying, "It just isn't necessary to be so miserable. Why don'tcha wake up and have a ball, or at least live with some kind of dignity or something." Now that may sound like a protest but I don't think of it as a *protest*, I'm trying to shake people up a little bit and say, "Look, you don't haveta worry about that, it just isn't *important*."

MODERATOR: Do you feel that a poem has any special characteristics which need correspond to the traditional list that you're all so well acquainted with, or is there something else, something transcendent about a poem, which to you is the beginning and end of its definition?

WHALEN: Sure. The connection or whatever you want to call it—is to music, as far as I can see. Not necessarily to metric, or to anything else, except as it relates to a *musical* experience, a musical feeling, in the line, happening between the words, or happening as the poetic line— it's a musical . . .

WELCH: Right. Right.

WHALEN: . . . shot for me, and that's what I *hear* when I write. And that's what I hear in a lot of the most interesting poems that are being done now.

WELCH: Robert Duncan gave me a very good phrase the other night. He said when you read a poem, you "play the poem." And this is very important to me. In a way, my style of reading out loud, *performing* a poem, is a very— is something I *practice*. I practice how I think the line should be played. And I spend a great deal of time getting the thing to swing, to flow, to *move*, as the line was written. You see, as you write the line you're writing a *movement*, like a musician is writing a movement, or a dancer is dancing one. My objection to the academic poets is they seem unnecessarily limited. Why limit yourself to a ten beat line? Why not write a fifty beat line? Or a two beat line? Or whatever you need.

MODERATOR: Do you write your poems to be heard?

WELCH: I always do, yes. Cause I think of it as speech. Always.

SNYDER: To go back just a second to what you said a second ago, Lew, why not write a fifty beat line or something . . .

WELCH: Unh-hunh.

SNYDER: I think the point to that is simply that the old forms just don't work anymore for us and that we are working toward something new.

WELCH: Right. We really are.

SNYDER: But we're finding—*feeling* our way into something that is not clearly established, and maybe it never will be, but the demands of poetry now are different than they've been in the past, and to try to write in the traditional modes of English poetry is to bend something around where it won't work anymore.

WELCH: Yes, and it's not that technical either. The *mind* of the present time is not the mind of the past.

SNYDER: Exactly.

WELCH: Mr. Pope's mind was a very orderly, rational one that liked to put things in little boxes. And so for him the rhymed couplet is a perfect expression of his mind. I'm trying to get out of the inside of my head some kind of a wordless shape, and I take that shape and I try to put it into words, and the result, if I'm successful, is a poem. Then I look with the same kind of discovery that any reader would, I say, "Oh, that's what the shape is," and it may be very weird, some sort of a thing I've never seen, with a chunk in the middle that looks like what we used to call prose or some such thing, or it might look like a funny list, or there might even be a picture drawn in it, or whatever. I give myself the right to use anything at hand to try to get this thing out of my head.

WHALEN: Well, that's very funny because the idea of having a shape in your head that I try to fit words to is the way I write *prose*.

WELCH: Oh.

WHALEN: I wrote a whole novel that way last year and it's very entertaining. Nobody likes it. [Laughter.] In any case, it satisfies me and it worked out that way—I worked from that "stance," as Olson would call it. But I don't think—I think that you guys are making it a little bit too hard. I think that the poetical experience is there since prehistory, and we've still got it, and the thing about the shape of it, or what not, isn't terribly important. I think that the . . .

SNYDER: Well, what I *mean* is . . .

WHALEN: . . . the poem is still happening and . . .

SNYDER: Sure . . .

WHALEN: . . . we drop in and out of it.

WELCH: Yeah, that's true.

SNYDER: But the poetical experience at different times and different places seems to demand a different form, and to try to take what is the pure poetical experience and throw it into iambic pentameters is to maim it.

WHALEN: Oh, yeah, all right, so . . .

WELCH: And that's all we meant.

WHALEN: If you don't do it very well, it surely will.

SNYDER: If you do that *now*—?

WHALEN: Oh . . .

SNYDER: Maybe not. Sure.

WELCH: But you see, I think. Well I know for a fact, just looking at Dryden or Pope, I know they were doing the same thing we are. It just, you know, the experience of writing for them was probably absolutely identical. I don't see any reason why it would be any different. They have something to say and they sit down and they sing it.

SNYDER: Well, I think that Dryden and Pope are not very good examples for that.

WELCH: I think Dryden is because his forms are very spon—uh, seem to me—there's a nice roughness about some of his poetry that gives me the idea it was a very inspired work, that he really just blew like a jazz musician, like his "A Song for St. Cecilia's Day," for example . . .

WHALEN: Yeah . . .

WELCH: . . . are just gorgeous things.

WHALEN: And the "Secular Masque," for instance, is great.

WELCH: Yes. Uh, Pope isn't a good example, you're right there. That seems to me unin . . .

MODERATOR: You can't set Pope to jazz . . .

WHALEN: No, but he's doing something else, he's doing something else . . .

WELCH: He's doing something else, sure. Beautifully, too.

WHALEN: . . . and he's doing it with a much different aim. I mean his idea of perfection and correctness is something else—he's a really inspired poet. Byron tells you right in the preface to one of his poems about how Pope is a great writer, and why, and what's the matter with everybody for neglecting him, and so . . . That's one of the big shots about college. I have *no beef* against college. At least when I went there Lloyd Reynolds turned us on to Pope, and said, "For gosh sake go read this guy because he's a great technician," and we went and dug . . .

WELCH: Yes. Sure. I never would have found Dryden if it wasn't for that funny professor that just loved him so much, he'd just . . .

WHALEN: But then we went and dug . . .

WELCH: And there it was.

WHALEN: . . . and there it was, and it happened.

WELCH: Real good stuff.

WHALEN: But then, of course, if you just sit and take notes, I don't suppose anything will happen. But that's the student's fault, I think.

WELCH: Or if the professor doesn't really care. Often . . .

WHALEN: Yeah. That's true.

WELCH: . . . he doesn't really care. So if—like Cocteau once said, "A work of genius demands a public of genius . . ."

WHALEN: Well . . . [laughs]

WELCH: . . . to some extent or other. It really does. I mean a work of genius, especially in the hands of a teacher, requires real genius on that teacher's part, or the kids are just going to get completely turned off. Like most kids by the time they get out of high school have been very carefully taught for twelve years that they will *never* understand poetry. And they believe it the rest of their lives, some of them. And then some of them find that this ain't true.

WHALEN: On the other hand, another classmate of ours, Bill Dickey, is teaching at State College this past couple of years. I'd sure love to have been in on his eighteenth-century course. I bet . . . [laughs] talk about turning people on, I'll bet he did it good.

WELCH: Yeah. I'll bet he did it very well. Yeah, yeah.

MODERATOR: Do you think that the university offers a haven for poets?

SNYDER and WELCH [overlapping] : No. Certainly not for me. I just—there's a—for me, there's just too much critical, uh, the funny analytical mind, critical mind, is just everywhere. You can't get away from it at a col—even when you try to have a cup of coffee. And there's a good mind, a mind that I like to play around with, and everything. But I like the poetic mind better, and I find I do way, way better if I stay very far away from the academies on principle.

WHALEN: It's great fun to visit, and they pay me to visit them [laughs] . It's very nice.

WELCH: I love to visit universities and read before student audiences. And they're very stimulating audiences, wonderful people.

WHALEN: Yeah. And it's great to talk to the kids . . .

WELCH: . . . and the professors, it's great to talk to. Yeah.

WHALEN: . . . who are interested. They're very lively guys.

MODERATOR: What do they seem to want to know?

WHALEN: They want to know how—they ask the questions that you did.

WELCH: The same questions.

WHALEN: "How do you get along? What—how—did you go to school? Did you stay in school? [Laughter.] Should I go out and hitchhike up and down America? Shall *I* get a job washing glass?

WELCH: "Shall I be a poet even though I'm a girl?" Things like that, you know. And . . .

WHALEN: Yeah, yeah. Those are all very important questions to 'em, and they worry about them.

MODERATOR: Well, do they ask you questions about poetry?

WELCH: Oh yeah. "How old were you when you wrote your first poem?"

MODERATOR: But that's getting back to you again.

WELCH: "Is this a poem?"

WHALEN: But then they very seldom say . . .

WELCH: Oh, yeah. They ask that . . . Go ahead, Phil, sorry.

WHALEN: Something very funny happened last summer at this huge conference in the University of British Columbia up in Vancouver. Ginsberg told me that he and Creeley got there the first day to open up the first session and they didn't know what to *say* to the huge audience of waiting kids, and he says, I asked Bob Creeley, I said, "How do you write, do you use a pencil or a fountain pen?" And Creeley says, "Well . . . "—and he went, he just took off—[laughter]

WELCH: Yeah.

WHALEN: —"I have this pencil, see, and I have a pencil sharpener, and I have this eraser that I've had for the last nine years . . . "

WELCH: Yeah.

WHALEN: " . . . it's only about this big now." [Laughs.] And he went on, and finally he said, "And then I take that, and I sit there and I write in the morning."

WELCH: Yeah, yeah.

WHALEN: And Allen says, "Well, now, I carry a fountain pen, or just a ballpoint pen right now that I got in Japan," and so forth—rattle rattle rattle—he was going on, and they really got down . . .

WELCH: Sure. That's right.

WHALEN: . . . to the basic thing that writing is a business of sitting down and writing.

WELCH: And writing words down on a piece of paper. Of course.

WHALEN: And it's because you've got a call to say something. You do. It's a call.

WELCH: Yeah. What's that favorite quote of yours from Mr. Walpole? "I write to relieve not the emptiness of my purse, but the fullness of my mind." [Laughter.] I always thought that was a beautiful thing to say. So there you are with your mind all packed and you unpack by writing it down on a piece of paper and then you go out and just live like anybody else, you know.

SNYDER: Well, that's one way . . .

WELCH: Yeah. There are a lot of ways.

MODERATOR: Yes.

SNYDER: I get the feeling that the students ask us rather different questions than they ask their professors.

WELCH: Yes, I do too, and I think . . .

WHALEN: And the professor could answer them perfectly well if a student felt like asking him, and apparently they don't.

WELCH: Yeah.

SNYDER: I don't think the professors know the answers to those questions sometimes.

WELCH: Some of them do but they've forgotten in the complexity of their art—teaching is a very complex art— they sometimes forget the very basic, simple little questions that are really underlying everything. I think—I know it's good for me to talk to professors, and I think it's good for professors to talk to poets, and I *know* it's real good for the kids. It's quite different seeing Dr. Williams, for example, standing before you for the first time reading his poems. It was an *enormously* important experience for me when I was twenty-four years old, an experience from which I never recovered. It was a very beautiful thing. And suddenly you realize what poetry is about. It's not something that's in a library somewhere: it's something that comes out of a man.

MODERATOR: Gary Snyder, you're going to be teaching at the University of California next fall, is it?

SNYDER: Yeah. Fall semester.

MODERATOR: What are you going to be teaching? What do you want to do?

SNYDER: Well, I don't have any choice in the matter, particularly, but what they're going to have me do is just fine with me. Apparently, I'm going to be teaching one upper division creative writing poetry class and a couple of lower division freshman composition classes.

MODERATOR: Is this going to put you in the role of a critic?

SNYDER: I don't think so. At least I won't be criticizing anything that I don't feel naturally like criticizing. I don't have any feeling that this is going to be difficult because I'm called upon to function as a poet.

WELCH: Yes. Now see that's quite different than being called upon to function as a teacher.

SNYDER: Well, a poet-teacher . . .

MODERATOR: You're going to be asked to evaluate, presumably.

SNYDER: Oh yeah. Well, I have my own ways of evaluating. Now they may not be quite the same ways of evaluating that are used commonly in the academies, but my ways work too, and they can be explained a little bit, I think.

MODERATOR: What criteria would be operative?

SNYDER: In looking at a poem and judging it?

MODERATOR: That's right.

SNYDER: Well, the first thing would be the sound of it. Does the person know how to throw the words around, and does it sound right when read aloud. Then the second would be a psychological and moral thing: is the poem straight? Does it—is it phony, or is it straight? Is it true, or is it lies? And does it gear in with what I think is necessary and proper in modern poetry, or is the fellow trying to pull something out of a tradition which isn't his. In other words, does it come from the man himself and not from a book. Little things like that.

WELCH: Yes, yes. I don't see any reason why this should be necessarily true, but the fact is that very few writers that take full time jobs with universities keep on writing, or write as well as I think they would if they hadn't done this. I don't know why this is necessarily true, but it almost always is. But there is now coming a new thing in universities, I think is wonderful—poets in residence, poetry workshop things, and so on, that you can go into and stay for a couple of semesters and then leave. And I think that's a very healthy thing.

WHALEN: Yeah.

WELCH: It's good for the poet, I know. Very good for him—very stimulating. And I think it's good for the academy too because it keeps it kind of from getting into ruts, and getting boring. It's a pretty lively thing when Mr. Auden comes to your campus, and he marches around that way. And then next year, maybe Phil Whalen comes. And next year: *Corso* comes. And then it's all very wild and alive that way, you see, for both the poet and the academy. And the kids then get an accurate view of what this art is all about.

SNYDER: I'm pretty interested, actually, in what's going to happen teaching at Berkeley this fall. I've knocked around and had so many different kinds of jobs by now that a job is a job. And I'll get paid a better wage than I do when I work in the engine room of a ship as a wiper. Now I might be able to do a little more writing in the engine room of a ship, but . . .

WELCH: Um-hm.

SNYDER: . . . working eight to twelve hours a day, six days a week, is pretty exhausting, in its own way.

WELCH: Sure.

SNYDER: So, talking to these kids is going to be fun in its own way. And fine. Let's go, you know.

WELCH: Yeah.

MODERATOR: When you give public readings, do you find that the atmosphere is a kind of spontaneously exciting thing that generates your best, as opposed to—well, this kind of public reading: I know that you have one coming up on June 12th where the three of you will be reading your poems ... Let's take the kind of reading where you're working this way, as opposed to a more formal lecture situation. I guess you've all been the college route ...

WELCH: Yes. Um-hm.

MODERATOR: ... and stood up on a stage in front of a large group of students, and more or less been asked to read, and there wasn't this interaction that I know takes place in some of the San Francisco readings.

SNYDER: But you can do it ...

MODERATOR: Oh yes.

SNYDER: ... Like I read just last Friday at Berkeley, and the thing is you're not a teacher, you're a poet when you stand up there.

WELCH: Exactly.

SNYDER: Within five minutes you've got the kids going with you on that level, or you're not a poet.

WELCH: Well, that's part of your job. Yes.

SNYDER: Yeah.

WELCH: You can spot a poet just that way. If the kids sit there bored—they're probably right, they're probably listening to a bunch of boring stuff that doesn't much matter to them.

SNYDER: What you're there to do is to break through to the human being in everybody.

WELCH: Exactly.

SNYDER: So that's what you do.

MODERATOR: What about the other readings—who turns out for the San Francisco readings? What kinds of audiences?

WELCH: A *wonderful* audience. Everybody comes. Not a great *many* of them, but every conceivable kind of person, it's a—I think it's the best, well certainly the best audience for poetry I've ever seen. I've read in New York, and I prefer to read around here. It seems to be a very warm, responsive audience. And sometimes it really gets very carried away—there's cheering and stamping and screaming and . . . I remember when I was a kid, or in the forties, poetry readings were awful *grim* things. Nobody ever got *excited* at one. They'd sort of sit there and dream or something.

MODERATOR: It was kind of an intellectual salon atmosphere that you had?

WELCH: Yeah. Now it's more like the atmosphere that happens when good jazz is being played.

MODERATOR: What about the relationship between poetry and jazz? It's been discussed to death, but maybe we can deal a few last . . .

WELCH: I feel—in my work, they're very closely connected. The kind of music I naturally think in is jazz music. And so the music that comes in my poetry—I sometimes deliberately try to write a poem that moves around like Monk's music, if the subject matter, you know, connected with that kind of rhythm.

WHALEN: He's one of the greatest musical geniuses [laughing] . . .

WELCH: Oh, he's just great . . .

WHALEN: . . . that this country has produced.

WELCH: It's a very challenging thing to try to do in words . . .

WHALEN: Nobody pays any attention to him.

WELCH: . . . Yeah.

WHALEN: He's a great man.

SNYDER: Well, sure. Jazz is one of the revolutionary things of this century. Like Confucius said, "When you change the modes of the music, the society changes."

WELCH: Yes.

SNYDER: And what we are in the middle of right now, is one of the biggest cultural changes that's taken place since the Neolithic. With a . . .

WHALEN: I hope so.

SNYDER: yeah . . . Well, I think it's true.

WELCH: We sure need it. [Laughter.]

WHALEN: Yeah.

SNYDER: . . . with a whole new consciousness on the verge of being born . . .

WELCH: Yeah.

SNYDER: And jazz is one of the things that's doing that.

WELCH: Sure.

SNYDER: So that like I can't do—I don't know the music well enough to do anything, like Lew says, deliberately. But I know that the rhythms and the sounds that are playing in my subconscious are jazz rhythms.

WELCH: Sure.

SNYDER: And they affect the line that I write.

WELCH: And that's one of the interesting things about the difference between New York and San Francisco. There's a big, tough, uptown sound to people like Charlie Mingus, and so on, and there's another sound that comes out of, oh, musicians like Desmond, and something—oh, a more lyric, less frenzied, *cool*, and very beautiful thing that comes out of the West Coast jazz. And I think that's true of the poets too. I know some of that New York poetry is very beautiful, but gee it's so *fierce*, you know, and it *has* to be, because, you know, that's a *tough* town.

MODERATOR: What're you thinking of specifically?

WELCH: Oh, I think, like the difference between Whalen's poetry, say, and LeRoi Jones'. Or the difference between *Howl* and my poetry, say, where a . . . it's definitely caused by the fact that Allen grew up in that awful, wild town, and I grew up in these relatively gentle, sometimes sound-asleep *bland* little West Coast towns, you know.

MODERATOR: Well, you're saying then that like the difference which exists between New York jazz or Kansas City jazz . . .

WELCH: Right.

MODERATOR: . . . or Chicago jazz and San Francisco jazz, there's also regional differences in *poetry*.

WELCH: There have — there always will be.

MODERATOR: Do you all agree with that?

WHALEN: To a certain extent, it's true.

WELCH: But it's not very important, ultimately.

WHALEN: I don't think it's an interesting difference.

WELCH: No, finally I . . .

SNYDER: We move back and forth a lot.

WELCH: Sure.

SNYDER: I talk more about horses and mountains . . .

MODERATOR: So do the poets . . . right.

SNYDER: . . . and mules and axes and things in my poetry . . .

WELCH: Yeah.

SNYDER: . . . than anybody in New York would . . .

WHALEN: Yeah.

SNYDER: . . . but those are the things I've grown up with.

WELCH: Sure. And then a—you know some of the concerns of a—it's interesting how the idea of writing spontaneously has been kicked around quite a bit—Kerouac being the big champion of that, his statement being that he never changes a word at all, and so on. But we all write—I think we all are thinking someway or other about a spontaneity, a jazz-like blowing of the line, not only when you perform it but when you actually write it, which results in the same kind of excitement and surprises, if you get to do it right. Suddenly you find you're *way off* here, and you didn't even think you were gonna get there, and now you gotta get back. And you'll hear trumpeters doing that, and so forth. In other words, I find there's a *very similar mind* in this performing jazz man, and the one that I have when I'm a performing or writing poet.

WHALEN: I don't know, I think that we're all getting to sound *terribly* stuffy— [laughs]

SNYDER: I do too.

WHALEN: I mean the three of us are sitting here like we were *embalmed* or something—but I wanted to say. I made this list before I came . . .

WELCH: OK.

WHALEN: . . . to tell you all that we have successors, and this is very nice: that in New York there's a magazine called *C*, edited by Ted Berrigan and Ron Padgett, who are *very* interesting young poets . . .

WELCH: Good.

WHALEN: . . . who don't have that hard uptown sound. They're doing a funny thing—they're taking off from Gertrude Stein.

WELCH: Yes, yes . . .

WHALEN: Lorenzo Thomas is doing that.

WELCH: That high wit thing . . .

WHALEN: And then other young persons that are happening like that are here in town. There's Joanne Kyger, who has a tone of her own. George Stanley and Stan Persky have their own funny music going—still heavily influenced by their teachers, Duncan and Spicer and Robin Blaser, but still doing . . .

WELCH: Yes.

WHALEN: . . . having some funny, new breakthrough. John Wieners, in the East, is on a *totally* different level.

WELCH: Exactly.

WHALEN: And much younger than we.

WELCH: Yes.

WHALEN: And McClure is just functioning like, like . . .

WELCH: Yeah.

WHALEN: . . . he's got a new book out, *Ghost Tantras* is out right now. Lamantia has gone underground again, but I sure want to see what he's done when he comes up . . .

WELCH: You know damn well he's not silent . . .

WHALEN: . . . [laughing] comes out again.

WELCH: . . . under there.

WHALEN: And up the coast a ways, still up in Washington where he's raising dogs—James Koller is a sculptor and poet who's writing very well. So there's a lot more happening, thank God. I mean . . .

WELCH: Than it sounds like from what we're just saying. Yeah.

WHALEN: . . . the whole load isn't entirely on me, and that —or on us, or on you.

WELCH: Yeah.

WHALEN: And that's real great.

SNYDER: No, this is a social thing that's moving forward and what's going to be happening fifty years from now will be someplace different.

WHALEN: Yeah, yeah.

WELCH: I think we all have to remember to thank Dr. Williams. That poor guy carried the *whole* load . . .

WHALEN: Oh, I don't think so.

WELCH: . . . or practically all of it for years and years.

SNYDER: I don't think he had the whole load.

WHALEN: No, no.

WELCH: Well, he carried a lot more of it than any one person seems to be carrying right now. Because there is *so* much activity going on now.

SNYDER: Then there's kids up in Vancouver, British Columbia, too . . .

WHALEN: Yeah, yeah.

SNYDER: . . . that run that little mimeographed magazine *Tish*.

WHALEN: Yeah, yeah.

SNYDER: George Bowering . . .

WELCH: Well, San Francisco State is just full of very hard working . . .

WHALEN: There's all kinds of activity there, yeah.

WELCH: . . . young writers and writers our age.

SNYDER: So, something of the same thing is even going on in Japan. There's a group now of writers around that fellow Sakaki that are wandering the countryside and managing somehow to have some kind of an international view of life and of the world, instead of just being hung up on what it is to be a Japanese, and are writing in a new kind of language—and at the same time *being* Japanese, living in the countryside.

WHALEN: And that's another thing—is that all of us are known probably more widely in Europe [laughs] than we are in Berkeley!

WELCH: Sure.

WHALEN: I imagine that people pick up their radio and tune in KPFA and say, "Well, who are these guys?" you know. Whereas our work is translated into Swedish, German, Italian, Spanish, I dunno—who [laughs] —it's very funny . . .

WELCH: Some of it showed up in Nicaragua, somebody said . . .

WHALEN: Yeah.

WELCH: . . . in a pirated edition.

WHALEN: Yeah.

WELCH: Some little revolutionary organization thought we could help them shoot their bad enemies, or whatever.

WHALEN: And the best . . .

WELCH: I, for one, was real delighted.

WHALEN: Yeah, that's very . . .

WELCH: I just hope people like that keep stealin' it.

WHALEN: That's very important to me—to think about, you talk again about audience, or to come back again to your thing about what audience do you visualize—I think it's just great to be able to reach out and hand a great bouquet to some cat in Poland or . . .

WELCH: That's right.

WHALEN: . . . or Italy, or South America, or Japan, or someplace else—"Hi, there!" you know. But they *get* it— but it does get *through* all the nonsense and blather and advertising, and so on. It does go directly to some other person and not just in the next county, or back home in Oregon, but to Milan, where I have a pamphlet coming out very soon, or to China, or wherever else.

MODERATOR: Our radio audience is even more mysterious than an audience at one of your readings because we have no idea who is out there.

WELCH: Right.

MODERATOR: But in tying this up, is there anything finally that you'd like to say to that mysterious collective entity called our audience?

WHALEN: I want to read this thing called "The Double Take," which is something about that.

THE DOUBLE TAKE

I want leeway
I want room to move
November tree with scarlet flowers
Don't crowd me
Bluey-green distant hilltops a picture
I know it comes out of the water
Angel Island the foot of Steiner Street

Admit these pleasures
Ordinarily unseen, I accept them
      demand more

And I need space and time away from you
Demand more, higher quality
I can't stand to look at you,
Hear what you say, watch how you behave
Your insolence, your ignorance

I must have distance,
Isolation, silence,
A vacation from your monstrous beauty

My infinite lust for you.

WELCH: Oh, that's very good.

WHALEN: So I'm glad to see you, but I also want a distance, and you can read it.

WELCH: Right. OK. Or hear us.

MODERATOR: OK. We can actually quit now unless anybody else has something. Anybody have a poem? Any . . . [laughter]

WELCH: I hadn't planned on it.

MODERATOR: I happen to have a poem . . . [laughter]

WELCH: Sure. I got two . . .

WHALEN: Just happen to have brought my violincello . . . [laughs]

WELCH: . . . two great big boxes full of 'em here. But I don't know, gettin' kinda hot and tired . . .

MODERATOR: OK.

WHALEN: I think the water jug is empty [laughs] .

GREY FOX PRESS BOOKS

Edward Dorn — *Selected Poems*

Allen Ginsberg — *The Gates of Wrath: Rhymed Poems 1948-1952*
Gay Sunshine Interview (with Allen Young)
Chant Mantra Poetics

Frank O'Hara — *Early Writing*
The Fourth of July, A Novel
Poems Retrieved
Standing Still and Walking in New York

Charles Olson — *The Post Office*

Gary Snyder
Lew Welch &
Philip Whalen — *On Bread & Poetry*

Lew Welch — *How I Work as a Poet & Other Essays/Plays/Stories*
I, Leo—An Unfinished Novel
Ring of Bone: Collected Poems 1950-1971
Selected Poems
Trip Trap (with Jack Kerouac & Albert Saijo)

Philip Whalen — *Decompressions: Selected Poems*
Scenes of Life at the Capital